THE MERCHANDISE MART

A BUILDING BOOK FROM
THE CHICAGO
ARCHITECTURE FOUNDATION

JAY PRIDMORE

WITH PHOTOGRAPHS BY
HEDRICH BLESSING

Pomegranate

SAN FRANCISCO

Published by Pomegranate Communications, Inc.

Box 808022, Petaluma, California 94975

800 227 1428; www.pomegranate.com

Pomegranate Europe Ltd.

Unit 1, Heathcote Business Centre, Hurlbutt Road

Warwick, Warwickshire CV34 6TD U. K.

(44) 09126 430111

Library of Congress Cataloging-in-Publication Data

Pridmore, Jay.

The Merchandise Mart : a building book from the Chicago Architecture Foundation/ Jay Pridmore ; with photographs by Hedrich Blessing.

p. cm.

ISBN 0-7649-2497-4 (alk. paper)

1. Merchandise Mart (Chicago, Ill.) 2. Graham, Anderson, Probst, White. 3. Art deco (Architecture)—Illinois—Chicago. 4. Chicago (Ill.)—Buildings, structures, etc. I. Blessing, Hedrich. II. Chicago Architecture Foundation. III. Title.

NA6233.C4M476 2003

725'.2'0977311—dc21

2003051164

Pomegranate Catalog No. A688

Book design by Monroe Street Studios Santa Rosa, California

Printed in Korea

10 09 08 07 06 05 04 03   10 9 8 7 6 5 4 3 2 1

EAS

MISSION

The Chicago Architecture Foundation (CAF) is dedicated to advancing public interest and education in architecture and related design. CAF pursues this mission through a comprehensive program of tours, lectures, exhibitions, special pro-grams, and youth programs, all designed to enhance the public's awareness and appreciation of Chicago's important architectural legacy.

Founded in 1966, the Chicago Architecture Foundation has evolved to become a nationally recognized resource advancing public interest and education in Chicago's outstanding architecture. Its programs serve more than 350,000 people each year. For more information contact us at the address below, or visit us on our website:

Chicago Architecture Foundation
224 South Michigan Avenue
Chicago IL 60604
312-922-TOUR (8687)
www.architecture.org

Acknowledgments

Special thanks to members of the staff of Merchandise Mart Properties, Inc., including Executive Vice President Christopher Kennedy, Joanna Mannino, Monica DeBartolo, and Jennifer Woolford.

Hedrich Blessing was unstinting in assembling photographic images, especially ones of the restored interiors. To Mike Houlahan and Bob Shimer, heartfelt gratitude.

The Chicago Historical Society generously helped assemble photographs from their Photographs Collection and the Hedrich Blessing Collection, the historical archive of Hedrich Blessing, which resides at the Historical Society. President Lonnie Bunch, Director for Collections and Research Russell Lewis, and Rights and Reproductions Coordinator Rob Medina were most helpful.

Tony Jahn, Archivist Historian of Marshall Field's, helped research photographs and archival documents about the Mart when it was the property of Marshall Field & Co.

At the architecture firm of Booth Hansen and Associates, Larry Booth and Lori Carmichael assisted in recounting and illustrating recent developments in the interior of the building.

At the Chicago Architecture Foundation, the efforts of Zurich Esposito, Vanessa Oltmanns, and President and CEO Lynn Osmond were most appreciated. Editor Edward C. Hirschland of The Landhart Corporation was indispensable. Thanks also to Bonita Mall, formerly of the Architecture Foundation, who helped bring the Building Books series into existence.

CHRONOLOGY

1927 James Simpson, president of Marshall Field & Co., announces that Field's will build the Merchandise Mart for the wholesaling of merchandise to retailers nationwide.

1928 Air rights—a new concept in Chicago—over the Chicago & North Western rail yard are purchased for $2 million.

1930 The Mart is completed, at a total cost of $32 million.

1936 After the Great Depression, Field's gives up its wholesale and manufacturing businesses. The Mart is almost empty; its largest tenant is the federal government.

1946 Millionaire Joseph P. Kennedy purchases the Mart for a reported $16 million. He makes the Mart a national marketplace for the furniture and design industries.

1950 The first Good Design exhibit is mounted at the Merchandise Mart, organized jointly by the Mart and the Museum of Modern Art in New York.

1969 NEOCON is inaugurated as a yearly market event for the contract furniture industry.

1991 A major renovation of the Mart involves its public spaces on the first two floors and corresponds with the development of the River North neighborhood behind the Mart.

1999 The Kennedy family sells the Mart to Vornado Realty Trust and invests heavily in Vornado. Christopher Kennedy, grandson of Joseph Kennedy, stays on as executive vice president of Merchandise Mart Properties.

INTRODUCTION

Few buildings in America are as imposing as the Merchandise Mart, a Chicago landmark not only for its size but also for the unique and striking character of its architecture. When built in 1930, the Mart was known as the structure with the most floor space in the world; less obvious was that it would define, as few buildings could, the streamlined Art Deco style that symbolized the prosperous, stylish decade in which it was designed.

Although now surpassed in size by other buildings, the Merchandise Mart still dominates its stretch of the Chicago River, and with some impressive raw numbers—4.5 million square feet in floor space (nearly equal to the Sears Tower) and more than 7 miles of hallways. It still goes by an old moniker, the Colossus of Marketplaces.

But more important than sheer mass, the Mart's profile, especially when illuminated at night, is an unmistakable presence on Chicago's skyline. Today its classic-modern design contributes immeasurably to its fame—it attracts scores of tenants dedicated to furnishings and up-to-date architecture—and to its longtime function as the world's largest design center.

The building's long-term success would gratify the creator of the Merchandise Mart, James Simpson of Marshall Field's, and its principal architect, Alfred Shaw of the firm Graham, Anderson, Probst and White. Indeed, the Mart was one of the most carefully designed buildings of its time. Its massive size was neither accident nor megalomaniacal caprice. The Mart was

Completed in 1930, the Merchandise Mart was designed by Graham, Anderson, Probst and White, architects responsible for many of Chicago's great monuments.

The site was key. Chicago, regarded as the epicenter of American commerce, was integral to the Merchandise Mart concept. And it was built directly over a railroad, the better to transport goods. Today, the Mart occupies a place on the river that continues to draw attention from many different viewpoints.

Conceived in 1927 at the height of the country's prosperity, the
Merchandise Mart was constructed to be the world's largest commercial
building. It also had designs on being one of the most glamorous.

While Chicago's big-shouldered warehouses are an obvious influence, a taste for handsome detail also connects the Mart's architecture to Chicago's department store tradition.

envisioned as advancing Chicago's ambition to become the largest city in the world, and it was built in a time when "goodness could be found in bigness," as historians have characterized the era of big business, big government, and big ideas that marked America's emergence as a great world power.

The Mart represented a definite advance in Chicago's revolutionary role in the development of commercial architecture: a brilliant example of the multiuse structure. The idea that large buildings could serve many purposes was pioneered during the late 1800s in Chicago's Loop, where offices, stores, theaters, hotels, and many other features were designed into single structures. Indeed, the Mart carried the multiuse idea several steps forward. As a blend of several building types, including the warehouse loft and the early steel-frame skyscraper, its success owes largely to the adaptation and refinement of several canons of the Chicago School of Architecture, established in the late nineteenth century by a group that included William Le Baron Jenney, John Wellborn Root, Daniel Burnham, and Louis Sullivan.

Today, the Mart is not often counted among the most dazzling gems of Chicago architecture, but few buildings in the United States have a design so closely suited to its complex function. The "form follows function" dictum—

first stated by Sullivan and still the sine qua non of Chicago architecture—is a fundamental standard by which the Merchandise Mart can be judged, and judged favorably, in the twenty-first century.

Wholesaling Center of the World

In 1927, the management of Marshall Field & Co. announced the idea for the Merchandise Mart, which primarily would be a headquarters for the firm's vast wholesale divisions, the backbone of the organization. Yet it would serve more than Field's needs alone; the Mart would open its vast marketplace to hundreds of other wholesalers. Based on Chicago's position as a transportation center and the city's seemingly limitless future, the idea was to make the Mart the wholesaling center of the world.

The Merchandise Mart would typify "an age of increased efficiency through consolidation," as a Field's executive explained at the time. It also stood to reason that civic development would follow the business model: the principle appeared to have developed naturally in other sectors of Chicago commerce—State Street had developed into a retail magnet, and LaSalle Street became the banking center of the West. Chicago would now have a new mecca for store buyers.

It did not work out that way, unfortunately. Field's once-dominant wholesale business had been losing money since 1920, and the burden of the company's bottom line depended on its magnificent State Street department store.

The wholesale divisions, previously located in the Marshall Field Wholesale Store, a now-demolished architectural landmark in the Loop designed in the 1880s by Henry Hobson Richardson, grew rich when the West was young. But now, cities and towns in the hinterlands were growing, and bigger stores there were buying direct from factories rather than traditional middlemen. Field's management believed that the downward trend in wholesale could be reversed with a bigger wholesale operation, one that was consolidated with the competition. The strategy behind the Merchandise Mart never had a chance, however, thanks to the Great Depression.

Yet the failure of the Merchandise Mart was not permanent. When Field's sold the building in 1946, its new owner, Joseph P. Kennedy, accomplished many of the goals of Marshall Field & Co. The Mart became a thriving center for many wholesalers. It also became a civic monument and an architectural anchor in a part of the city that had not been much to look at previously. It demonstrated that architecture does not just reflect social and economic condition—it has the positive power to encourage and effect change.

The Mart went up at a time when many local architects were turning their backs on the Chicago River. Yet its design celebrated the river, with a broad esplanade and the beginnings of a boulevard drive.

Photograph Bob Shimer
© Hedrich Blessing

The idea that shopping boulevards could be constructed indoors—"rainless streets," as Mart management described their building—was a new idea when Marshall Field's conceived and constructed a national wholesale market.

The idea for the Merchandise Mart originated with one of the most powerful men in Chicago. James Simpson, Field's chairman since 1923, advanced through hard work and utter self-confidence. Sometimes called an empire builder, he also possessed immense energy and the conviction that to rush forward with bigger, more daring plans was the road to success.

Simpson possessed another quality that was typical of many Chicago business leaders at this time: civic-mindedness. As the powerful chairman of the Chicago Plan Commission during the middle to late 1920s, he applied his sharp business acumen to the business of making Chicago grow, which it was doing at an unprecedented pace. Although the Plan Commission was appointed and not elected, and its decisions were advisory and not law, Simpson clearly took his planning responsibilities seriously.

Generally, Simpson's objective was to advance the 1909 Plan of Chicago, the late Daniel Burnham's idealistic scheme for a city with the splendor of European capitals. It called for public projects like boulevards, bridges, and parks to set the city's architectural tone and style. Then, according to the plan, private interests would follow with buildings of appropriate design and grandeur, creating a complete and harmonic city fabric. Although some members of the economic elite as well as politicians were blind to overall social needs, Simpson and like-minded citizens politically engineered many enduring public works of Burnham's plan. He negotiated with railroad executives to clear their rail yards and straighten the South Branch of the Chicago River. He

Courtesy Marshall Field & Co.

James Simpson (right) was president of Marshall Field's and chairman of the
Chicago Plan Commission when he broke ground for the Merchandise Mart.
His intention was to revive the flagging wholesale side of the business with a
colossus that would attract store buyers from all over the country. He also
believed that the Mart advanced Chicago's bid to become the world's
largest and greatest city. Shown with Simpson is 88-year-old John Griffiths,
head of the contracting company Griffiths & Son, which built the Mart.

Earlier renderings of the Merchandise Mart by Graham, Anderson, Probst and White had a more traditional style and were more reminiscent of the Wrigley Building design than the Art Deco design that was finally used.

Courtesy Marshall Field & Co.

The Mart would be a great central market and a center of transportation with a new "North Bank Drive," envisioned to connect Michigan Avenue to the east with the never-built Avondale Highway that was proposed to run northwest from downtown Chicago.

oversaw the completion of Wacker Drive and helped promote the construction of major skyscrapers to line it.

Thus it was natural for Simpson to have larger designs for the Merchandise Mart than the mere interests of the company he headed. The Mart was designed for enterprise and also as a civic monument. It was the architectural manifestation of Simpson's image of Chicago as the world's "Great Central Market," the title of a 1921 advertising piece that Simpson created for the store. This publication reflected Simpson's belief that the destiny of his company was inextricably linked to the destiny of Chicago. On some levels, it meant that what was good for Field's was good for Chicago. But he also believed the converse. Thus, the Merchandise Mart represented a brilliant addition to the riverfront, a grand monument and a much-needed addition to a neglected corner of the city near the Loop. Plans even included a mirror image of Wacker Drive to run along the river's north bank. Whatever good fortune Field's would generate in creating a wholesale market would advance Chicago's objective of becoming the largest, greatest city in the world.

Simpson lost the battle to revive his company's wholesale business. Nor was the boulevard on the river completed. But the grand idea behind the Merchandise Mart was sound and even powerful. After World War II, new owners of the Merchandise Mart created a thriving central wholesale market, smaller in scope but of the kind that Field's intended. The massive multiuse building became a splendid fixture on the riverbank, dominating its section of downtown Chicago much as the Plan Commission's chairman hoped it would.

Photograph Chicago Aerial Survey Co., courtesy Marshall Field & Co

The north bank of the Chicago River's main branch was largely undevel-
oped in 1927 when Marshall Field & Co. announced plans for the construction of the Merchandise Mart on the trapezoidal rail yard at left.
Field's president, James Simpson, envisioned a building to rival the pyra-
mids and a boulevard to match Wacker Drive across the river.

The rail yard continued to be used for local freight service, even after the Merchandise Mart rose up above the tracks (shown here), serving Marshall Field's scheme to create America's great central market.

In one of more than 400 caissons sunk to bedrock along the river, Simpson
and others share a light moment at the construction site. The man driving the
loader thought better of dumping the rubble on Field's powerful chief executive.

The first step in creating the Merchandise Mart was to identify and acquire a site to suit its massive form and complex function. Simpson chose the old rail yards of the Chicago & North Western Railway at Wolf Point—once the site of the railroad's main terminal—where the Chicago River turned north. These yards were now used for freight. The property was sold through a land-use technique brand-new in Chicago: "air rights."

The idea was to purchase the right to build over the railroad tracks, a concept that had been used successfully over trackage at Grand Central Station in New York a few years before. The idea was also being used for a site for the new Chicago Daily News Building (completed in 1929) just west of the river on Madison Street. While the purchase of the railroad's air rights for the Merchandise Mart would be the world's largest transaction of the sort, the transaction was not expected to be a problem. Business wanted it. Labor wanted it. Most importantly, the Plan Commission wanted it, explaining that among its advantages, it would hide the unsightly view of working rail yards in the "City Beautiful."

Only the Illinois Commerce Commission stood in the way, leading to suspicions that its members had not been sufficiently bribed. (The Mart was planned at $18 million and ended up costing twice that.) Ultimately, positive public pressure was too much, so the Commerce Commission finally agreed, whereupon Marshall Field's paid the railroad $2 million for air rights along with deeds to more than 400 separate parcels where caissons were to be sunk to bedrock to support the building's foundation.

Courtesy Marshall Field & Co.

Track was laid on the Mart's construction site while the foundation was being poured, partly to facilitate deliveries of the steel posts and beams that were used in the structure of the Mart, along with thousands of tons of poured concrete that were delivered by barge.

James Simpson's son, in the foreground, March 1929, drives a rivet into the ironwork of the building. He was a director of Field's and later a member of Congress.

Courtesy Merchandise Mart Properties, Inc.

There was some doubt that the dirigible was absolutely essential in the construction of the poured concrete structure. In all likelihood it was enlisted to call attention to the building, which was probably unnecessary, too.

The firm of architect Ernest Graham was quickly chosen to design the new Merchandise Mart. No other really emerged to compete, as Graham, like his mentor Daniel Burnham, was thoroughly identified with values that had originally inspired the idea for the great central market. Both Burnham and Graham were not just architects but builders as well, especially skilled in helping clients conceive large, expensive schemes, then coaxing those projects along.

Like Burnham, design director of the 1893 World's Columbian Exposition, Graham was an organizer par excellence, beginning his career under Burnham as construction superintendent for the great Chicago fair. But whereas Burnham was an idealist who imagined a city of sparkling boulevards and majestic vistas, Graham was much more the realist. During a period of immense prosperity, he presided over a practice, following Burnham's death in 1912, marked less by architectural reflection and more by sheer impatience to build.

Graham, Anderson, Probst and White (GAPW)—the firm that succeeded D. H. Burnham & Co.—became Chicago's leading architects for a period that extended at least through the depression. Partly because of Burnham's legacy but largely because of Graham's no-nonsense approach to business, GAPW had been chosen to execute many of Chicago's most important commissions in and around the Loop, including the Field Museum, Union Station, Civic Opera House, and the completion of Marshall Field's State Street store.

11-21-29
46727

As the Mart went up in 1929, 2,500 workers were employed for the duration of the project. They used nine cranes atop the building to lift steel and other building materials. Hoists running up the sides were for concrete that was ready to be poured.

GAPW, which had 300 employees at its height, was not an organization for risk takers. In many cases, its designs could be interpreted as having come directly from an elaborate architectural pattern book and superimposed directly on the Chicago Plan template. The Field Museum's elaborate classical form, for example, represented a "climax to an urban vista," as Sally A. Kitt Chappell noted in her book, *Transforming Tradition: Architecture and Planning of Graham, Anderson, Probst and White, 1912–1936.* Comparing the building to the Louvre in Paris and Piazza Venezia in Rome, Chappell wrote, "the Field Museum gives monumental form to South Lake Shore Drive."

Union Station was similarly planned, situated directly between the commercial and industrial districts of Chicago and was a grand portal to the Loop. Grandly classical, it provided what Burnham said a rail station had to provide: not just a train stop but a space for "those public ceremonials that take place in front of the gateway of a city."

Eventually, GAPW designed buildings without direct prototypes, mixing styles as a way to create bigger and more profitable structures. One of its most successful was the Civic Opera House, a multiuse project that housed offices and an opera theater. Completed in 1929, its theater became one of grand opera's greatest venues. Above, it was a simple, unadorned skyscraper.

Similarly, the Merchandise Mart was planned not only as the world's largest commercial building, but also as a highly complex multiuse structure. It would be a warehouse, but it would also be a department store and a commercial

The Mart's design followed the conventions of the early tall building. Although it had the dimensions of an industrial warehouse, it also featured the base, shaft, and capital that signified the classic American skyscraper. The sign at right claims that the Merchandise Mart is "The Largest Building in the World."

office tower. Indeed, GAPW and its principal designer at the time, Alfred Shaw, had already mastered the canon for each type of building, and they were in a position as no other firm to execute an original and ultimately graceful blend of the three.

Curiously, the Merchandise Mart's architecture was little discussed as the building was planned—much more interesting was its size, "a city with a permanent population all under one roof," as one publication described it. But its design was a modern classic. It featured the elements of a commercial skyscraper—vintage 1920s—with a central tower projecting slightly from the mass of the building, and long, uninterrupted piers, setbacks, and a pyramid-shaped roof emphasizing its height. Toward the top were fifty-six acroteria (later removed) of Native American chiefs that were too small to be seen from street level but were visible from the windows of other tall buildings across the river.

The Mart's resemblance to another classic building form, the Chicago School loft, was also critical to the design's success. Indeed, the Mart's appearance as a big-shouldered warehouse—albeit a stylish one—marks the building as eminently practical and functional, which it strove above all to be. In many ways, the building's most striking characteristic is its sense of proportion and grace, handed to the Mart's designers directly from Jenney, Root, Holabird, and other Chicago School luminaries.

Other elements of the design were borrowed from another type with many antecedents in Chicago, the large department store. For example, luxurious

Photograph © Hedrich Blessing

A massive building that might have been a graceless box took on a stream-lined aspect with its trapezoidal footprint, curved turrets at the corners, and a central tower with the vertical setbacks characteristic of the Art Deco era.

Thoroughly modern buildings were often elaborately illuminated, and none to more dramatic effect than the Merchandise Mart, shown here in the 1930s.

display windows framed in bronze lined three sides of the building at street level. Inside, the corridors on the upper floors were called business boulevards, whose traffic flow, color selection, and "scientific" lighting were drawn from GAPW's experience as architect to retailers, not just Field's but Gimbel's in Philadelphia and others.

Mainstream Modernism

Department store imagery was largely responsible for the modern Art Deco lines that tied together varied elements of the building. Nascent modernism in the Merchandise Mart inspired its curved or "chamfered" corners on the exterior and its distinctly flat surfaces. Shaw was certainly wedded to architectural precedent, but he also had one foot resolutely in a modern architecture of sleek geometric forms without the heavy ornament traditionally drawn from history.

Modernism was a debatable subject at the time. In 1927, for example, it flared up at a meeting of the city's Association of Arts and Industries, where Alfonso Iannelli, a sculptor who had worked with Frank Lloyd Wright, replied to the remarks of a conservative society decorator: "It is as silly for us to build our Field Museum, stadium and aquarium in classic Greek architectural style as it would [be] for us to issue our daily newspapers in the language of classic Greece." Graham, Anderson, Probst and White bridled but saw the writing on the wall. Fashionable interiors of the day were modern, and so were the selling spaces of department stores, which made their living by reading future trends.

Courtesy Chicago Historical Society

The geometric style of Art Deco ornament inspired fifty-six Indian chiefs as acroteria on the twenty-second and twenty-fourth stories of the Mart tower. Sadly, they were torn out in a 1961 renovation and replaced with "clean-looking concrete," as described at the time.

The Mart's interior space exhibits a size and a dynamism that hark back to Chicago's earliest multiuse buildings. The Merchandise Mart logo in the terrazzo floor (above) was used throughout, as both a decorative feature and to identify the Mart as an institution in and of itself (facing page).

When the Mart was renovated in 1991, its space became an up-to-date indoor shopping mall in the up-and-coming neighborhood of River North. Yet its split-levels and walkways above were echoes from the Art Deco era, styles rarely matched in late-twentieth-century shopping centers.

The Merchandise Mart Guide Service was instituted in 1948 to satisfy general interest in a building that was filled with consumer goods but largely closed to the public.

Courtesy Marshall Field & Co.

Among five different restaurants in the Mart, the lunch counter was claimed to be the longest in the world.

At Field's, modern decor was everywhere, largely because their head designer, Arthur Fraser, was an avowed modernist whose abstract window displays were the talk of State Street. As the store's house architects, GAPW could not ignore the tendency to streamline traditional designs, and so in the Merchandise Mart the firm found the largest canvas to date for Art Deco architecture (sometimes called Art Moderne).

Shaw's use of the Art Deco style proved that new and modernistic architecture was moving into the mainstream and could be gracefully incorporated into the city's design. The Mart's lobby, for example, features eight square marble piers, each slightly fluted to suggest classicism, but in this case angular, stripped-down versions of the Beaux-Arts models that prevailed when the Field Museum, for example, went up just a few years before. Doors and fixtures of retail shops and restaurants were then—as now—bright in color and geometric in form. The lobby's murals, by artist Jules Guerin—who illustrated the 1909 Plan of Chicago—display historic subjects of commerce around the world in a distinctly modern style, with layers of color and lavish use of gold leaf.

Depression and Recovery

Like many classic commercial structures, the Merchandise Mart has been declared obsolete several times. The first was shortly after its completion in 1931. In the midst of the depression, Marshall Field's wholesale business declined with the rest of the economy—many of its wholesale lines were

With NBC's headquarters on the nineteenth and twentieth floors, public interest in the Mart only grew. Tour guides, increasingly popular, were the building's most public representatives.

Nineteen separate paintings in the frieze around the main lobby constitute "a panorama of the world's commerce and industry," a local reporter noted shortly after the murals by Jules Guerin were unveiled. Switzerland is represented because of its watchmaking industry.

Minarets and the dome of St. Sophia are in Guerin's mural of Istanbul,
known among the world's merchandisers for its precious rugs and textiles.

As Chicago modernized in the 1960s, the Merchandise Mart was nearly forty years old, but it appeared up-to-date, along with modern trains and the futuristic Marina City.

The Merchandise Mart, streamlined and spacious, made an attractive setting for America's new consumer culture and its Technicolor view of the world in 1951.

discontinued in 1936—which meant that the store possessed a nearly empty building and a mortgage for most of its costs. During World War II the Mart was partially filled with military and government offices, but they never paid the high rents—nor had the sparkle—envisioned in the original plan.

James Simpson, the Mart's creator, died prematurely in 1939. By 1946, Field's management was eager to leave the real estate business now that the firm was no longer in wholesale. That year they sold the Mart to millionaire Joseph P. Kennedy—former ambassador to Great Britain and father of a future president—reportedly for $16 million, about half of what it had cost to build. Kennedy was a shrewd investor, having sold most of his large stock portfolio well before the 1929 crash. He had a knack for management, too, refining the Merchandise Mart according to Simpson's idea of nearly two decades before.

Kennedy understood that the Marshall Field concept required too radical a change in how merchandise was wholesaled. Salesmen, Kennedy believed, resisted remaining in a showroom and waiting for customers. But they would sit down for something more transitory; with that in mind, Mart managers organized trade shows in many of the traditional merchandising categories—linens and menswear, for example—and aggressively convinced manufacturers to attend. Mart shows became an alternative to the less formal markets held in hotels, where salesmen rented rooms and had buyers in for a look.

Thus the Merchandise Mart played a central role in the development of the trade show industry and in making Chicago its natural epicenter. Other venues

A 1951 kitchen had every modern convenience, including a double stainless steel sink. The view from the window is of course not real; in fact, another part of the Mart is beyond the wall.

Stereo was new in American homes in 1961. Clairtone Sound Corp. promoted it in a Merchandise Mart showroom as part of the latest design elements for the home.

Joseph Kennedy's objective when he purchased the Merchandise Mart was to attract corporate tenants as well as wholesalers. While the NBC studios already occupied the tower, Quaker Oats Company arrived after the war, and by 1969, when this photograph was taken, exhibited the latest trends in corporate design.

The Merchandise Mart was distinctly modern when it was built, but with the passage of time its design became a classic of its era. In the Mart's 1991 renovation, a walkway to the Apparel Mart next door features geometric form that recalls the Mart's Art Deco origins as well as its pervasive functionality—the glass reflects outside heat and light to help keep the passage cool during the summer.

Photograph © Hedrich Blessing

Recent changes and improvements at the Mart have revived the
sleek and uncluttered lines of its 1920s-modern origins.

and other cities could and did eventually draw this business away. But then in the 1950s, the Mart sharpened its focus on the sector that it would dominate for decades. The postwar furniture industry was booming but also changing, and by the 1960s, manufacturers were selling less through big furniture stores and more through new channels like designers and architects. For such "non-stocking" retailers, spacious showrooms, wide corridors, and an ample freight infrastructure made the Merchandise Mart the perfect place to conduct their wholesale business.

Kennedy also worked to arouse public curiosity in the Mart with a trained team of uniformed guides conducting tours of the otherwise closed building. In 1953, he added the Merchandise Mart Hall of Fame, honoring America's greatest merchants, such as Marshall Field and F. W. Woolworth, based on the idea that the commerce carried on at the Mart represented a social force more important than the simple pursuit of a salesman's next order.

Kennedy originally stated that he purchased the Mart based on his faith in Chicago. His strategy also demonstrated faith in architecture and design. Both impulses paid off from the beginning. In 1950, he made the Mart an unmistakable point of reference in the furniture industry with the Good Design exhibits, a joint project with the Museum of Modern Art in New York. As wave after wave of new products for the home flooded the market, the Good Design exhibits established a bridge between commercial industry and artistic design. With the imprimatur of MOMA and its curator, Edgar Kaufmann, ex-apprentice

Courtesy Chicago Historical Society

In 1954, a rooftop celebration dinner capped installation
ceremonies for the Merchandise Mart Hall of Fame.

Earlier that evening, busts of Marshall Field, John Wanamaker, George Huntington Hartford, and Frank Winfield Woolworth were unveiled along the river parapet. The Hall of Fame, created by Joseph P. Kennedy, was intended to celebrate America's merchants, "without whom the mass producing of goods would be pointless," as Kennedy explained.

Courtesy Marshall Field & Co.

Among the bronze heads in the Merchandise Mart Hall of Fame was that of the founder of the company that built the Mart, Marshall Field I, second from left. The final inductee among eight now honored on the Mart's esplanade was Aaron Montgomery Ward, in 1972.

to Frank Lloyd Wright and heir to a Pittsburgh department store fortune, Good Design became a sharp selling point for the products included in the semiannual event. It also promoted the Merchandise Mart's profile as a towering arbiter of design.

Good Design lasted five years. Later, in 1969, another cultural and commercial event was inaugurated at the Mart with NEOCON, an annual convention for designers and manufacturers of business interiors. As with Good Design, the Merchandise Mart had the size to give NEOCON the critical mass that such an international event needed. Just as important, the Mart's pervasive Art Deco design rendered these events with the élan and glamour that they required for success.

By the early 1990s, the Mart faced other changes. Two major corporations that had been tenants for decades departed, moving to sleek skyscrapers named for them. But the distinctive architecture of the Mart continued to attract other major office tenants. Rents derived from spacious corporate offices, important to the success of the Mart from the start, remain fundamental to its economic viability today.

And as its form remains adaptable and appropriate for many uses, its function seems likewise endlessly adaptable. It handles trucks in the former rail yard underneath the building as naturally as it serves as a commercial office building with a measure of prestige. It has housed interior designs of countless architects and designers—Richard Meier and Thomas Beeby in the showrooms, for example, and Helmet Jahn, who designed a pedestrian overpass

In 1942, the Old Hickory Furniture showroom sold traditional household furniture with bold touches that foreshadowed modern trends and that would mark the featured styles of the Mart in years to come.

Hedrich Blessing Collection, Chicago Historical Society

over Orleans Street to the Apparel Mart. In 1991, the first two floors were renovated with stylish retail shops. They contributed to the redevelopment of
Chicago's River North, once a gritty warehouse district behind the massive bulk
of the Mart, now transformed with expensive lofts and other signs of glittering
life in the shadow of the most stylish loft building of them all.

Taken together, the latter efforts were telling as a demonstration of the
Merchandise Mart's protean strength and dominating presence in Chicago,
and as an integral and functional work of architecture. While many of its
strengths in the twenty-first century were unknown when the Merchandise

Mart was designed, it remains
a building of unique functionality that has succeeded in
redefining itself several times.
It is a sign not just of architecture's ability to reflect its
times, but also that there are
certain absolutes in architecture—classical proportion,
multiuse function—that made
Chicago a great architecture
center and the Merchandise
Mart one of the city's most
enduring monuments.

Photograph © Hedrich Blessing

In 1991, the firm of Booth Hansen created a showroom for Haworth Inc. They referred to the place for technology and people as a "mixing bowl." The architects said that the existing Mart structure of white rectilinear columns "engages a dynamic relationship with the overlapping curvilinear 'message walls' creating ease of movement and active visual experience."

Opposite: Major architects who design showrooms continue to demonstrate Chicago's continued importance. The office of Krueck and Sexton created this undulating glass wall for Herman Miller in 2001, at the end of which they placed Charles and Ray Eames's Time Life chairs, icons from the 1950s.

The Mart's north side was dotted with service entrances when built. But the River North area just outside became a fashionable loft neighborhood, and a new Kinzie Street entrance and lobby were made suitable for limousines.

A Union Jack flew to celebrate the opening of the British government's new trade office in the Merchandise Mart. It was a step forward in the Mart's efforts to create a center of international commerce and communications.